IMAGES
of Sport

IPSWICH TOWN
FOOTBALL CLUB

Skipper Mick Mills (left) and star Dutchman Frans Thijssen pour champagne into the UEFA Cup in 1981 to start dressing room celebrations after the victory over AZ 67 Alkmaar in the final. It was one of the great moments in the history of Ipswich Town Football Club. Copyright Eastern Counties Newspapers Group Ltd.

IMAGES
of Sport

IPSWICH TOWN
FOOTBALL CLUB

Compiled by
Tony Garnett

TEMPUS

First published 2000
Copyright © Eastern Counties Newspaper Group, 2000

Tempus Publishing Limited
The Mill, Brimscombe Port,
Stroud, Gloucestershire, GL5 2QG

ISBN 0 7524 2152 2

Typesetting and origination by
Tempus Publishing Limited
Printed in Great Britain by
Midway Clark Printing, Wiltshire

Also available from Tempus Publishing:

Forever England: A history of the national side
Lords – The Cathedral of Cricket
The Five Nations Story
The Football Programme: A history and guide
Speedway in East Anglia

Contents

The Mayor of Ipswich, Dr P. Weiner, welcomes manager Alf Ramsey (second left) and the Ipswich Town players who won the Division Three (South) Championship in the 1956/57 season. Looking at the shield are, from left to right: Neil Myles, Ted Phillips, Roy Bailey, Billy Reed, John Elsworthy, Dai Rees, Ken Malcolm, Tom Garneys, Jimmy Leadbetter, Basil Acres and chairman John Cobbold. Note the half-full pint of brown ale that no one had remembered to clear away before the picture was taken. There was no sign of champagne at this Town Hall event.

John Cobbold was Ipswich Town's chairman between May 1957 and May 1976 when he handed over to his younger brother Patrick. John was the youngest director in the Football League when he was appointed to the board in November 1948 at the age of twenty-one years and four months.

Introduction

Football means so much in the lives of so many people that the arrival of the professional game in Ipswich in 1936 was long overdue. It's amazing that almost fifty-eight years elapsed between the formation of the Ipswich Association Football Club on 16 October 1878 and the decision to leave the amateur ranks.

The first president of the football club was, almost inevitably, a member of the Cobbold family. Thomas Clement Cobbold, a great-great-uncle of recent chairmen John and Patrick, was Tory MP for Ipswich between 1876 and 1883 when he died at the age of fifty. Ironically, the big rivals of the day were the Ipswich Football Club (who played rugby) and whose home was at Portman Road. It was not until 1888 that the clubs merged and the footballers grew stronger and the rugby players weaker.

Many people would say that there was no floodlit football in Ipswich until 1960 – but on 17 December in 1878 on a snowbound pitch at Brook's Hall (also off Norwich Road), United Suffolk beat Ipswich 5-3. It was a gamble that backfired; it was reported that 'several prominent businessmen lost money on the venture'. Tickets were not cheap – 1s 6d for a reserved space bought on the day down to sixpence for an unreserved ticket bought in advance. Teale's conveyances, we are told, ran from the Cornhill to the ground at five-minute intervals so there was plenty of pre-planning to make the night a success. However, early lessons about the dangers of over-pricing when trying to sell to a discerning Suffolk public were plain for all to see. The lights, though, were the main attraction. Ransomes, Sims and Head, who had played a leading part in lighting the Thames Embankment by electricity, loaned two six-horsepower engines, one of which won a Gold Medal at the Paris Exhibition. These worked the brilliant Siemen's dynamo-magnetic light. This demonstration of the powers of electricity was far more important than the actual match. There was back-up from Bunsen battery lights and it was a spectacular show – but too few people turned up to balance the books.

Ipswich School provided the bulk of those early Town players and the opposition was provided by the likes of Framlingham College, Woodbridge Grammar School, Harwich and Colchester Town. The autumn of 1880 was important. The legal brains of two of the club's players, Stephen Notcutt and George Sherrington, who were also solicitors, set up the amalgamation with the Ipswich Football Club. Portman Road, where there was a 'better surface', became home. In those days the practice pitch area was used. The area where the main pitch is today was still wasteland with trees growing on it. At first Ipswich took part only in friendly matches. They had five seasons in the Suffolk Challenge Cup before deciding to try their luck in the FA Challenge Cup for the first time in the 1890/91 season. In the first qualifying round Town beat Reading 2-0. Their next match was a 4-2 victory away to Norwich Thorpe (Norwich City were not formed until 1902).

There was a big decision at the start of 1894. The Southern League was formed and Ipswich was invited to take part. It was not until April 1895 that a meeting was held to discuss the matter, with the influential George Sherrington making the points in a letter to the EADT that 'overnight travel and professional opposition' would be involved. He said that the landlords of Portman Road 'may not wish professionals to appear there'. It seems he was wrong. Francis Peecock said that 'Football was played for fun – and was not to become a business' and there was considerable laughter when he said: 'Soon we shall be having Ipswich Town Ltd'. There was one lone voice in the wilderness, a businessman called R.D. Hendry who proposed that 'Ipswich Town should join the Southern League and employ a professional team'. The motion wasn't even seconded.

There were several Ipswich Town 'firsts' before the turn of the century. Ipswich had entered the FA Amateur Cup in the 1895/95 season and, having beaten the Old Harrovians 6-2, were drawn away to Bishop Auckland. They reached their hotel in Darlington by midnight and travelled third class – which surprised officials on the Great Northern Railway, who probably felt that all teams from the south were toffs. Ipswich lost 3-1, a marginally better scoreline than when they next visited this famous Northern club in an FA Cup third round replay in 1955 when Town, then in the Second Division, lost 3-0. Just imagine the excitement in Ipswich on Saturday 29 August 1936; Jimmy McLuckie, the illustrious former Scottish international secured on a free transfer from Aston Villa, was set to lead his side out in the new royal blue and white strip to face Tunbridge Wells Rangers. It was heady stuff, even against little known opposition.

Everybody involved in bringing professional football to Ipswich attended a pre-match luncheon at the Great White Horse, the most fashionable hotel in town in those days. A toast was proposed by Stanley Rous (later to become Sir Stanley) who was secretary of the Football Association and a Suffolk man. Captain 'Ivan' Cobbold, the Town chairman, responded. The band of the Scots Guards (Cobbold's regiment) paraded and Ipswich Town Football Club was launched with due ceremony. The fans did their bit as well – even though harvest was yet to be completed, there was a crowd of 14,211 on a sweltering day. The players responded with a 4-1 victory. George Dobson had the glory of scoring the Town's first professional goal. Jackie Williams, Bobby Bruce and Jack Blackwell added the others.

Winners of the Southern League title at their first attempt, Ipswich Town wasted no time in seeking election to the Football League. They felt they were good and ready, but the Town's first bid for League football met with disappointment. The tendency was for the 'old pals' act to protect the League clubs in trouble and, sure enough, Exeter City polled 40 votes, Aldershot 34 and Ipswich Town only 24. Chairman Cobbold was undaunted; he instructed Mick O'Brien to sign the best players available to make it very hard for the League to ignore Town's claims second time round.

Ipswich has had only ten managers since 1936. O'Brien did not last long because of an association with the married landlady of a Cobbold pub. Adam Scott Duncan was lured from Manchester United and it was largely his influence that helped Ipswich into the League. Alf Ramsey achieved the near impossible by guiding Ipswich to the Second and First Division titles in successive years between 1960 and 1962. As England coach he won the World Cup in 1966. Jackie Milburn took charge at a difficult time – who could possibly step into Ramsey's shoes? Bill McGarry, a strict disciplinarian, saw Ipswich back into Division One and almost immediately departed for Wolverhampton where there was 'more potential'. Then Bobby Robson arrived to transform Ipswich into a power in Europe before he also took the helm with England and his first-team coach Bobby Ferguson took over. John Duncan had a disappointing spell before John Lyall, once of West Ham, was headhunted to restore the club back to being among the elite. It was a hard job to compete in the Premiership and shortly before Christmas in 1994 Lyall announced his resignation.

His successor, George Burley, could not stop the slide out of the Premiership but gradually built his squad, despite financial restrictions, so that they returned to the big time after a Wembley play-off win against Barnsley in May 2000. There have been many great players whose exploits are recalled in the pages of this book. England captains Mick Mills and Terry Butcher, those crack marksmen Ray Crawford and Ted Phillips, and the Dutch masters Arnold Muhren and Frans Thijssen, are just some of the men who have brought joy to the people of East Anglia.

Who would have believed in 1936 that the country cousins from Ipswich would one day be rubbing shoulders with AC Milan, Real Madrid, Barcelona, Roma and Lazio? Who could have dreamed that they would one day win the FA Cup against Arsenal – the club that inspired Captain Cobbold to push for League football in the first place because of his friendship with the Hill-Wood family and a chance discussion at Alexandra Park races?

The story of Ipswich Town is breathtaking. This book cannot tell the full story, but hopefully the highlights will bring back many happy memories. My thanks are due to all the *East Anglian Daily Times* photographers over the years who have supplied the pictures and to Sharon Boswell who sorted out the negatives.

Tony Garnett
East Anglian Daily Times

One
The Early Years
1878 to 1955

The outside of Ipswich Town's fixture list for 1888/89.

The Ipswich Town team of the 1927/28 season who played in the Southern Amateur League. Many of the same players appeared at Wembley Stadium against Ealing the following season in the club's first ever match under the Twin Towers. From left to right, back row: Edwin Dutton (trainer), Reg Colby, A. Baker, G. Nicholls, Ray Colby, B. 'Tricky' Taylor, S.F. Fenn, Flight Lieutenant S.N. Webster. Front row: J. Green, L. Gibbs, W.V. Matthews, B. Chamberlain, C.W. Burch.

The club's fifth annual dinner and smoking concert was held on 27 March 1927 at the Limmer and Pipe restaurant in Buttermarket. This cartoon depicts the committee seated round the table with halos on top and has them hanging from the crossbar below. This seems a bit extreme until one discovers that in 1926/27 Ipswich Town finished second from the foot of the Southern Amateur League, were knocked out of the Amateur Cup in the preliminary round by Millwall United, went out to Lowestoft Town in the semi-final of the Suffolk Senior Cup and crashed 0-8 at home to Chelmsford City in the East Anglian Cup.

MENU.

SOUPS.

PUREE BRETONNE.

THICK GRAVY.

❧

FISH.

LEMON SOLES BERCY.

❧

JOINT.

ROAST SADDLE OF MUTTON.

VEGETABLES.   POTATOES.

❧

SWEETS.

PUDDING COLBERT.

MERINGUES AND CREAM.

❧

WELSH RAREBIT.

TOASTS.

Proposer.	To Respond.

H.M. THE KING.

THE CHAIRMAN.

Pianoforte Selection ...	MISS DOROTHY BRADSHAW.
Humorous Item ...	MR. HECTOR GORDON
	(Scottish Humorist).

IPSWICH TOWN FOOTBALL CLUB.

LT.-COL. F. W. TURNER.	MR. T. MULLINS.
Song	MR. ERIC SUTHERLAND
	Baritone.
Humorous Item	MR. WILBY LUNN.

THE TOWN AND TRADE OF IPSWICH.

SIR JOHN GANZONI, M.P.	
	COUNCILLOR K. J. BADSHAH, B.A., O.B.E.
	COUNCILLOR H. HOOPER
Humorous Item ...	MR. HECTOR GORDON.
„ „	MR. WILBY LUNN.

THE VISITORS.

MAJOR STUART. C.B.	MR. G. ROBSON,
	President, S.C.F.A
	MR. A. GIBB,
	Chairman, Westminster Bank
Song	MR. ERIC SUTHERLAND.
Humorous Item	MR. H. HOOPER.

THE CHAIRMAN.

| MR. ALAN TURNER. | |
| | MR. WILBY LUNN and his Marionettes. |

| Accompanist   ... | MISS DOROTHY BRADSHAW. |

Note that the dinner menu and toast list in 1927 has comedians and a baritone singer between the serious speakers that included the Member of Parliament, Sir John Ganzoni. It seems as though Mr Wilby Lunn and his Marionettes were on a hiding to nothing at the end of a heavy evening, despite the piano play of Miss Dorothy Bradshaw!

Left: Jimmy McLuckie, the Scottish international, who was signed from Aston Villa on a free transfer. This was considered a generous gesture by the Midland club because the player was only twenty-eight (although he looked older) and had cost Villa £6,500 from Manchester City two years previously. Bolton tried to entice McLuckie back into League football, but he remained loyal to Ipswich.

Right: On 10 November 1937, Ipswich was able to announce a managerial signing that surprised the football world. Adam Scott Matthewson Duncan, who still had three years of his contract to run with Manchester United, was persuaded to move to Portman Road. He was forty-nine years old. It should be pointed out, perhaps, that Manchester United in those days was by no means the giant it is today. They had just been relegated to the Second Division and Manchester City were the top dogs in the city. It is said that Captain Cobbold sent the United directors a crate of vintage port to seal the deal. Duncan was just the man Ipswich Town needed. He had friends in all walks of the game and his personal influence was crucial in securing the votes that led to entry into the League in the summer of 1938. Ipswich Town would never have been elected to the Football League at that memorable meeting in London on 20 May 1938 purely on the strength of coming third in the Southern League. The wheels certainly needed oiling and Scott Duncan was just the man to use his powers of persuasion. He was a popular and highly respected name in the game. Duncan, chairman 'Ivan' Cobbold and director Herbert Foster drove miles round the country to cajole League club chairmen into giving a vote for Ipswich. At the meeting itself the popular story, almost Ipswich folklore, is that 'Ivan' Cobbold said to Scott Duncan: 'We're not going to make it'. Scott Duncan replied: 'I bet you a sovereign we do and that we top the poll!' Captain Cobbold may not have been aware that Duncan had made successful last minute overtures to his old club Newcastle United to change their minds and support Ipswich. Five other clubs did the same. Duncan was proved to be right; Ipswich polled 36 votes, Walsall 34 and out went Gillingham with only 28.

Ipswich Town's biggest match at Portman Road in pre-war days was their FA Cup third round replay with mighty Aston Villa on 11 January 1939. Ipswich lost 2-1 before a then record crowd of 28,194. The picture shows pressure on the Ipswich goal defended by Mick Burns who had played for Preston North End in the 1937 FA Cup final. A crowd of 34,910 had turned out at Villa Park the previous Saturday to watch Jimmy McLuckie, a Villa old boy, and his country cousins from Ipswich force a 1-1 draw. Jock Hutcheson, signed from Chelsea the previous summer, was unable to play League football because he had already claimed insurance benefit for an injury. Hutcheson helped with training and was reserve team captain, but there was nothing to prevent him playing in the Cup. Hutcheson did not let Town down. Ipswich had wretched luck at Villa Park. Ambrose Mulraney was limping from the fifth minute. No substitutes were allowed in those days. Early in the second-half came one of the greatest controversies in the history of Ipswich Town Football Club. They were awarded a penalty. Charlie Fletcher was running up to take the kick when Villa full back, Ernest Callaghan, threw a lump of mud, which hit the ball, a split second before Fletcher's boot made contact. The Ipswich player's rhythm was momentarily disturbed. It was enough to save Villa. Fletcher's shot hit the post. Town's heated protests were in vain. It was a blatant case of 'ungentlemanly conduct'. When Villa's centre-half and captain James Allen headed the Midland side into the lead from a corner with seven minutes to go it looked all over. However, Town's never-say-die spirit shone through. In the 88th minute the Suffolk team was back on terms with a header from Hutcheson. It was euphoric for the visitors. Giantkilling was on the cards the following Wednesday but once again Ipswich suffered a cruel injury blow. Wing-half Dave Bell, who had been a key First Division player for Newcastle United, broke his leg after the interval. Ipswich had to battle on with ten men. Fred Haycock put Villa ahead. Ipswich summoned up all the courage they could muster and Fred Jones equalised after 74 minutes; Jones only played because of Mulraney's injury at Villa Park. There were only seconds remaining when Haycock struck the killer blow and Ipswich dreams were over. Even that goal was disputed. There was talk of handball and Town goalkeeper Mick Burns, normally so calm, chased the referee to the half-way line.

13

Left: Captain John Murray 'Ivan' Cobbold was club chairman when professional football was introduced at Portman Road in 1936. He was killed at the age of forty-seven when a German flying bomb struck the Guards Chapel in London during a service in June 1944. During the war debts had risen to £14,195. With the gates firmly closed at Portman Road, there was no income. There were several options open to the chairman. One was to put the company into liquidation and jeopardise all the hard work that had been done to win election to the Football League. The other was for the members of the board to dig deep and, between them, to pay off the overdraft so that they could start with a clean sheet when the war was over. The chairman was not prepared to see all his dreams for the club disappear. The money had to be paid. It may not sound very much now, but it was a daunting sum for anyone other than the very rich in the days when an Austin Seven cost £125. Colonel Harold Hooper, Herbert Foster, Nat Shaw and Robert Nevill Cobbold put in £250 each. Lord Cranworth, Sir Charles Bunbury, Hon Douglas Tollemache and Phillip Cobbold all contributed £500. This left the lion's share of the financial burden for Captain Cobbold, who by this time was a Lieutenant-Colonel in the Scots Guards but was still nicknamed 'Cappy' by the players. He paid a massive £11,195. His generosity was never widely reported at the time. His historic statement was poignant: 'As far as I can see there is now nothing to stop us re-opening football as soon as the war is over. I assure you that, if I am spared, I shall endeavour to get the club started again and producing reasonably good football as soon as possible.'

Right: Charlie Cowie, a centre-half who joined Town from Barrow in 1936, and was reserve team trainer from 1945 to 1965. He died on Christmas Day 1971.

In the summer of 1950, Ipswich Town appointed Jimmy Forsyth, a native of Bathgate in Scotland, as trainer-coach. Jimmy had served Millwall for twenty-four years, appearing in an FA Cup semi-final in 1937 when the Lions were the first Third Division club to get so close to Wembley. Jimmy had been assistant-trainer at The Den and was a fully qualified masseur and physiotherapist. Earlier in his career he had played for Portsmouth and Gillingham. He was to serve five different Ipswich Town managers before his retirement in 1971. In 1948 housing was a major problem for clubs and a frustrated Scott Duncan said: 'We could sign a good strong player straight away if we could find an unfurnished flat'. The newly-wed Matt O'Mahony asked for a transfer because he could not find a house and there was news from Plymouth Argyle that they had formed a housing society to buy property to let to players to encourage them to sign. To alleviate the problem in Ipswich, the Supporters Association purchased a house in Christchurch Street and rented it to players from outside the district. They called it Glemham in memory of the late chairman who had lived at Glemham Hall – the home of his widow, Lady Blanche, until she died in October 1987.

The front cover of the Ipswich Town Supporters' Association handbook for the 1949/50 season.

Dai Rees, a Welsh amateur international from Troedyrhiw, made his debut in April 1949 at the age of twenty-six. He made 387 first team appearances for the club and scored one goal. He had a long spell as club captain in succession to Tommy Parker. 'In these days of fantastic transfer fees, fancy figures are not necessarily the hall-mark of a good player.' Those were the words of wisdom spoken by Scott Duncan before the start of the 1949/50 season. The sentiments, of course, hold good today although Scott would never spend sixpence when threepence would suffice. The story goes that Scott was presiding over the team's breakfast at the Great Eastern Hotel in Liverpool Street Station after an overnight trip back from Plymouth on the night sleeper. He heard a coin drop under the table and was down on his hands and knees – just to pick up one penny. Ipswich finished eighth in 1950/51 season when the admission price was increased to 1s 6d and season tickets cost £5.10s. Cecil J. Robinson, a former referee and Suffolk County FA official, joined the board. Sammy McCrory ended top scorer with 21 goals with Ray Warne and Allenby Driver both in double figures. Dai Rees was ever-present with 48 League and Cup games. During the season Basil Acres, a full-back from Brantham, joined the staff. He had played for the Suffolk FA. At the end of the season Tom Garneys arrived from Brentford. Few who were there will forget the cry from the terraces 'Give it to Garneys'. In 1950/51 Ipswich won only two of their first nine games, which suggested another season of struggle. Then came a purple patch of seven matches in the autumn, which produced 13 points (out of a possible 14). The club enjoyed its best-ever run of away games between 30 September and 2 December, which brought six victories (one in the FA Cup) and a draw. There were no computers to blame in those days, but Ipswich had only one home game between 11 November and Christmas Day. Ipswich also forced a goalless draw away to champions Nottingham Forest: this was the first point Forest had dropped at home all season and the first time in twelve games that they had failed to score two goals or more. Pictured here in the early 1950s is trainer Jimmy Forsyth (right) with a group of first team players from the Scott Duncan era. From left to right: Tommy Parker (captain), Dai Rees, Jim Feeney (two caps for Northern Ireland), Neil Myles, Basil Acres and goalkeeper Jack Parry (one cap for Wales).

The promotion team of 1953/54. From left to right, back row: Billy Reed, Jim Feeney, Tom Garneys, Jack Parry, George McLuckie, John Elsworthy and Dai Rees. Front: Adam Scott Duncan (manager), Basil Acres, Alex Crowe, Tommy Parker (captain), Neil Myles, Tom Brown and Jimmy Forsyth (trainer). There were happy times at Portman Road in the 1953/54 season with promotion to the Second Division and a run in the FA Cup that took the club to the fifth round. The season started with four wins on the trot. A single point was dropped in seven matches and there were eight successive wins in a run of fourteen games without defeat between 16 September and 28 November. At the turn of the year Town were seven points ahead in the table (only two points for a win, remember) having used only thirteen players in thirty-one matches. Then injuries struck – the Cup run may have been exciting but it was also distracting – and, amazingly, seven defeats were suffered in nine games. For all the world it look as though a wonderful opportunity had slipped away, but doubters did not reckon with the character of skipper Tommy Parker and his men. Ipswich shook themselves down after a 6-1 Cup hammering in the fifth round at Preston (Tom Finney and all) and were unbeaten in their final ten games to pip Brighton and Hove Albion by three points. The previous season the defence had been pretty solid but this time round it was better still. Jim Feeney, forgetting his transfer request of the previous January, re-established himself at left-back. The stylish Basil Acres was at right-back with Jack Parry for once keeping injury-free – he played all forty-six matches in goal. Ipswich signed Billy Reed, a Welsh winger from Brighton, who played so well for Town that he won Welsh international honours against Scotland and Yugoslavia in 1955. Reed had been hailed 'the Stanley Matthews of the Third Division' and his signing was a masterstroke. George McLuckie (no relation to the great Jimmy who joined the club in 1936) was a twenty-two year old winger from Blackburn Rovers while Alec Crowe was an inside forward who had loads of experience with St Mirren. Tom Garneys was fit again and John Elsworthy's talent was becoming more obvious as the years went by. The final match of the season was a 2-1 win against Northampton Town after which J.W.H. Mears, chairman of Chelsea, presented Tommy Parker with the Championship Shield. On the Monday there was a civic reception for the players at the Town Hall and the following day came a tour of the town on an open-topped bus cheered by supporters who lined the streets. It all goes to show what a bit of success can do. The previous season the team had finished in sixteenth place and gates slumped, but now those stay-aways were back in force.

17

Left: Billy Reed was the first Ipswich Town player to win a full cap while on the staff at Portman Road. He was called up by Wales in 1955 for matches against Scotland and Yugoslavia, the latter game at Ninian Park in Cardiff. Although Reed played well he took a blow on his jaw and completed the game with concussion. He was sick and collapsed in the dressing room. He spent the night at St David's Hospital. Ipswich directors John Cobbold and Major Alfred Terry stayed in Cardiff to make sure all was well with their star player. Note the open terracing where the Britannia Stand now towers above the touchline. Up one season and down the next was the fate of Ipswich when they had their first taste of life in Division Two in the 1954/55 season. They found they were not strong enough to consolidate although, inspired as ever by skipper Tommy Parker, they put up a brave fight. Manager Scot Duncan thought his team would more than hold their own. In the first weeks of the new campaign no-one could argue with him. The season opened with a 3-2 defeat at the hands of Rotherham at Millmoor, which was no disgrace, followed by three successive victories. The first home match in the new division against Luton Town attracted 20,625. Tom Garneys had scored four goals in three games before Middlesbrough came to Portman Road for the return midweek game. It was amazing. The team from the North East were one up at the interval but Ipswich swamped them in the second half and ran out 6-1 winners with two more from Garneys, two from Alex Crowe and one each for wingers Billy Reed and George McLuckie. A Middlesbrough official was reported as saying: 'Your team will go far: just how far I hardly dare even suggest'. Who would have guessed on that happy night that Town's destination was straight back into Division Three (South)? The Boro match was followed by a run of ten successive defeats as Ipswich plummeted to rock bottom place. Wilf Grant, a twenty-nine year old, was signed in October in an effort to check the slide for a transfer fee of £7,500. He had previously been with Southampton and Cardiff City. The first game of that dismal run was a 4-2 defeat at Hull City when Garneys dropped out with back and groin trouble. Ted Phillips was promoted and scored both goals when up against none other than the famous England centre-half Neil Franklin. On the last day of the season Ipswich needed to win at Notts County and Plymouth had to lose at home to Stoke. Ipswich were caught on the break in the final minute but, as Plymouth won anyway, perhaps it's just as well that Town did not collect maximum points at Meadow Lane, they would have been inconsolable. The FA Cup saw an embarrassing defeat in the third round at the hands of the amateurs (shamateurs perhaps?) of Bishop Auckland.

Right: A notable departure in the summer of 1955 was goalkeeper Jack Parry, who refused reduced terms and joined Chelmsford City. Parry was a bricklayer and had worried Scott Duncan on a notable occasion when he was found to be on a roof pointing a chimney on the morning of an important match.

Two
Ramsey's Triumphs
1955 to 1963

Alf Ramsey, later Sir Alf, enjoys a joke with his goalkeeper Roy Bailey during a supporters' celebration after Ipswich Town's astonishing League Championship success. In the centre is proud chairman, John Cobbold. Reg Pickett, a former first-team captain, is in the background between Cobbold and Bailey.

Roy Bailey was signed just before the transfer deadline in March 1956 from Crystal Palace as cover for former Liverpool England B international Charlie Ashcroft, who broke his arm in a reserve match at Coventry. Bailey was soon preferred to George McMillan and went on to become an Ipswich Town legend.

A typical crowd scene at Portman Road at the start of Ramsey's reign. There are still plenty of cloth caps being worn. The summer of 1955 saw Scott Duncan stand down as manager. He continued as club secretary for three more years before retiring to Helensburgh on the banks of the Clyde. On 9 August it was announced that Ipswich Town had appointed thirty-five year old Alf Ramsey to be their new boss. The delay was because he had been coaching in Rhodesia. Ramsey was untried. It was his first appointment but he was renowned as a thinking footballer with 30 England caps. He had played at Tottenham under Arthur Rowe. Town director Nat Shaw, who owned the greyhound stadium in Ipswich, played a leading role in Ramsey's appointment. Ipswich were back in Division Three (South) after tasting the high life (for them at any rate) in the Second Division. The relegated Town players of 1955 took a wage cut which they accepted 'with disappointment but in the right spirit'. However, the board, under chairman Alistair Cobbold, had second thoughts at the end of October when the team had started to produce some good football; attendances were holding at around 14,500 and a 5-1 win at Reading had delighted everyone. The senior players' weekly wage was increased to £15 a week with a £2 win bonus and £1 for a draw. Mr Cobbold said: 'The directors are very pleased indeed with the football and in this way we are showing our appreciation'.

Tommy Parker switched to attack in 1956, beat Bill Jennings' scoring record of 25 goals by early March and looked as though finding the net had been his forte all his career. The popular captain totalled 475 first-team appearances in all, a figure that was eventually overtaken by Mick Mills. The picture shows Parker lighting a cigar for Mills, the first man to overhaul his appearance record for the club. Mills went on to make 737 first-team starts for Ipswich and had four outings as substitute. He won 42 full England caps, 5 Under 23 caps and was also a youth international. At the time John Duncan was appointed as Ipswich manager in 1987, Ipswich were refused permission to approach Mills who was then under contract as Stoke manager. Parker was never booked in his career. Hat-tricks, a rarity previously, came thick and fast in 1955/56 season. Parker (v. Swindon), Reed (v. Walsall), Grant twice (v. Millwall and Reading) and Tom Garneys (v. Northampton) all kept match balls. In the final weeks of the season Ipswich completed the double over Leyton Orient, the champions. The omens were good for the Ramsey era.

Before Ramsey arrived, Scott Duncan did him a big favour. He signed Jimmy Leadbetter (extreme right) from Brighton. 'Sticks', as he was to be affectionately known by Town fans, went on to win Championship medals in Division Three (South), Division Two and Division One. The picture shows the Ipswich front line that took Division One by storm. From left to right: Roy Stephenson, Doug Moran, Ray Crawford, Ted Phillips and Jimmy Leadbetter. Ramsey started on a low with a home defeat against Torquay United and only three points came from the opening four games as the new boss found his feet. He gave the players of the previous season the chance to prove themselves. Ramsey tried to sign Alex Forbes, the Scottish international, from Arsenal. The clubs agreed a fee but Forbes decided to stay in London. A slow start and occasional hiccups on the way meant that Ipswich missed out on promotion by a couple of points, but they were generally regarded as the classiest footballing side in the division and were highly entertaining. They scored 106 goals (previous best 82) and scored four goals or more in a match nine times. The 5-0 away wins at Northampton and Millwall equalled the club's record. Ramsey would almost certainly have led the club to promotion at the first attempt but for injuries to key players: Feeney (broken nose), Neil Myles (broken bone in hand), Billy Reed (cartilage operation), Wilf Grant (broken ankle) and Billy Baker (achilles tendon) all missed parts of the campaign.

In the 1956/57 season Ipswich Town hoisted themselves out of Division Three (South) never to return. Ipswich had retained the registration of Ted Phillips who had been released to play at Stowmarket in the Eastern Counties League. He returned to Portman Road to take the number 10 shirt from Tommy Parker. The other signing of note in the summer of 1956 was right-back Larry Carberry (pictured left leapfrogging over John Compton in training). Ramsey was starting to blend a useful side thanks largely to the strike force of Phillips and thirty-three year old Tom Garneys, who was second leading scorer despite missing a third of the season through injury. However, Ramsey was unsuccessful in his attempt to sign Dave Sexton from Leyton Orient. Billy Reed was sparkling on the wing, John Elsworthy was being tipped for Welsh honours and goalkeeper Roy Bailey was ever-present. With no points from the opening three matches and only three points from seven games, Ipswich made a slow start. The 6-0 victory over second-placed Torquay United in December lifted Ipswich from twelfth in the table to seventh. Dropped points at the end of March were worrying but then five successive wins saw them top the table on goal average with 56 points and two games to play. Being held to a 3-3 draw at home to Southend was a body blow but on the final day of the season Ipswich notched up a tremendous 2-0 win at Southampton with goals from Jimmy Leadbetter and makeshift striker Basil Acres. Even so, Ipswich had an agonising wait for the outcome of Torquay's match at Crystal Palace. It ended in a 1-1 draw leaving Ipswich as champions on goal average.

Ray Crawford (left) and Roy Stephenson in the thick of the attacking action against Norwich City at Portman Road.

Ipswich had a couple of seasons consolidating in the Second Division before the glory years started in 1960/61. Alf Ramsey had carefully blended a team that took English football by storm, his tactics of having deep-lying wingers Roy Stephenson and Jimmy Leadbetter baffling all the leading opposition managers and coaches. Ramsey's defenders are supposed to be having a tactical talk although it looks more like a posed picture. Goalkeeper Roy Bailey, Larry Carberry, skipper Andy Nelson, John Elsworthy and John Compton are on the practice pitch.

Ipswich Town started the 1960/61 season as one of the promotion outsiders, but Alf Ramsey's team proved them all wrong. The foundation was laid in the autumn with an unbeaten run of ten matches between 27 August and 15 October, with notable performances at Leeds and Charlton. The first major upset came when Billy Russell scored the only goal of the game to give Sheffield United victory at Portman Road. Shortly before Christmas the Blades had a six point lead whilst Ipswich had derby games with Norwich City, also promotion challengers, over the festive season. Two great victories for Town boosted confidence and a draw with Liverpool at Anfield was well earned. Then came the biggest test of all – a trip to Bramall Lane to play Sheffield United, who had just knocked Newcastle United out of the FA Cup at St James' Park. What a night it was in Sheffield. Goals from Ray Crawford (2) and Ted Phillips stunned the 35,000 crowd. Town were virtually in the First Division and imagine the excitement when promotion was clinched at home to Sunderland on 22 April. Chairman John Cobbold said: 'It has been the done thing in Fleet Street to tag Ipswich the "Cinderella club" but Cinderella is getting quite a big girl now, isn't she?' *Left:* Bill Baxter, then twenty-two, came into the Ipswich side against Norwich over Christmas when regular right-half Reg Pickett was injured. Although on National Service stationed at Aldershot with the Royal Engineers, he was given time to turn out for Ipswich and did the club proud. Alf Ramsey once said: 'I think he could play well in any position in the team'. But for Arsenal's Frank McLintock, Baxter would surely have won Scottish honours.

Right: The terrible twins, Ray Crawford (left) and Ted Phillips, whose goalscoring exploits became legendary. Crawford scored 40 goals in the 1960/61 season and Phillips netted 30. Known as 'Jungle Boy' because of National Service in Malaya, Crawford went on to play for England. Phillips, who now has two steel kneecaps, had the hardest shot in football. His powerful penalty kicks were feared throughout the land. Phillips was also a practical joker and always up to all sorts of harmless pranks.

In the big time at last. Ipswich Town's footballers find that autograph hunters are waiting outside their hotel. The players happy to oblige the youngsters are, from left to right: Roy Stephenson, Bill Baxter, Roy Bailey, Andy Nelson, Larry Carberry, Jimmy Leadbetter and Doug Moran.

Ipswich Town's first match in Division One was a 0-0 draw against Bolton Wanderers at Burnden Park, a ground that has been replaced by the Reebok Stadium. Ray Crawford is pictured in a tussle for a high ball. Eddie Hopkinson is the Bolton 'keeper (who played 14 times for England). Note the clock on the grandstand showing some quarter of an hour left to play. Ipswich stayed in the North West for the match against Burnley at Turf Moor the following Tuesday. They lost a cracking game 4-3 but it was one of the most exciting displays ever given by an Ipswich team. A week later Burnley lost the return match at Portman Road 6-2. When the season was over Ipswich were champions and Burnley runners-up. It turned into a dramatic season for Ipswich with all the top stars appearing at Portman Road. Ramsey's tactics were masterful – how else could a side made up of other clubs' rejects possibly take English football by storm?

Tottenham Hotspur had completed the Cup and League double in 1960/61. Bill Nicholson's side, captained by Danny Blanchflower, was generally regarded as the outstanding team in the land. On 21 October, the mighty Spurs came to Portman Road. They must have been taken aback by having to change in a converted cricket pavilion. They must have been shaken rigid by their 3-2 defeat. The Londoners led 2-1 at the interval but by the end Ray Crawford had scored twice and Ted Phillips once. The Ipswich deep-lying wingers, Roy Stephenson and Jimmy Leadbetter, had taken the country by surprise. Their supply of crosses enabled Crawford to score 33 League goals and 4 more in cups while Phillips scored 28 in the League and 8 more in cup competitions. The power of Phillips' long range shooting with the old leather ball was breathtaking. This picture shows the Tottenham goal under siege with Leadbetter hovering in the six yard box as goalkeeper Bill Brown tries to punch clear. In the return match at White Hart Lane Ipswich won 3-1 on a Wednesday night. On that occasion Phillips scored twice and Crawford once. Tottenham finished third in the table only four points behind Town.

Ipswich Town's well known mascot was 'Swede' Herring, a jovial bus conductor in the town, who turned up to home matches with his blue and white umbrella, which, in this picture, looks to have seen better days. 'Swede', with his booming voice, used to lift the crowd before the kick-off and was quite a character. Miss Switch, complete with her broomstick, was less regular as a mascot. The idea of making it a memorable day for one or more youngsters to kick around with the players and be present at the toss-up carries on to the present day.

'Swede' has his umbrella in good repair as the mascot of the day, armed with a wooden rattle, shows his prowess by leaping over the dugout. Some members of the crowd are watching the mascot, others have their eyes on the cameraman.

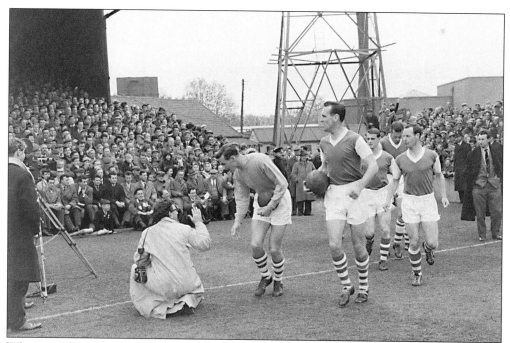

What is goalkeeper Roy Bailey saying to a photographer while running onto the pitch for a first team game? Skipper Andy Nelson looks round with Bill Baxter, John Compton and Ted Phillips behind.

Alf Ramsey recognised the role played by reserves. From left to right: Jimmy Forsyth (trainer), Wilf Hall, Roy Goulden, Reg Pickett, John Laurel, Derek Rees, Dennis Thrower, Dermot Curtis and Ken Malcolm.

The Championship-winning Ipswich Town team which kept injury-free for so much of the season. From left to right, back row: Larry Carberry, Andy Nelson (captain), Roy Bailey, Bill Baxter, John Compton and John Elsworthy. Front row: Roy Stephenson, Doug Moran, Ray Crawford, Ted Phillips and Jimmy Leadbetter.

The sight top goalkeepers came to fear. Ted Phillips cracks a left foot penalty past Wales and Arsenal goalkeeper Jack Kelsey at Portman Road. The game, which was played on Good Friday 1962, ended 2-2.

Roy Stephenson (centre) leaps to head the ball across the face of the Aston Villa goal in the final match of the season at Portman Road, which Ipswich won 2-0 to clinch the title. Ray Crawford is at the far post marked by John Sleeuwenhoek.

A section of the Ipswich crowd at the end of the 1961/62 season in front of Churchmans Stand. There are fans with rattles, visitors with Aston Villa favours, and a woman at the front complete with shopping basket.

Jubilant fans surge onto the field at Portman Road after Ipswich Town had defeated Aston Villa to become League champions at the first time of asking.

Trainer Jimmy Forsyth gets a celebration ducking in the communal players' bath. Jubilant Ipswich players are, from left to right: Jimmy Leadbetter, Roy Bailey, Ted Phillips, Larry Carberry, Ray Crawford and skipper Andy Nelson.

A moment to savour as Ipswich Town captain Andy Nelson holds the Division One Championship trophy high about his head outside the Town Hall. The players in the picture are: John Compton, Roy Bailey, John Elsworthy, Roy Stephenson, Larry Carberry and Jimmy Leadbetter.

The band played and well-wishers found precarious vantage points on the roof as Ipswich Town's champions passed the Post Office on their way to a reception at the Town Hall. Skipper Andy Nelson holds the trophy. The players, manager Alf Ramsey and chairman John Cobbold are waving to the crowds from the open-topped bus.

Supporters, many of whom had come in from the country districts (from where the club draws so much support) celebrate their team's success.

A pensive Ted Phillips, skipper Andy Nelson and chairman John Cobbold enjoy a glass of wine in the Mayor's parlour.

Ipswich played in the European Cup during the 1962/63 season. They started with the demolition of Floriana of Malta, 4-1 away and 10-0 at home (when Ray Crawford scored five). 'We must not delude ourselves that future rounds of the European Cup will be as easy as this one' were the cautious words of the manager. However, before the next round against AC Milan came the bombshell that Alf Ramsey was to succeed Walter Winterbottom as England team manager. It was raining throughout the match in the San Siro Stadium where only 7,607 turned up to watch the Italian stars take a 3-0 lead. This photograph shows Andy Nelson (right) winning a duel with the Brazilian Altafini.

Roy Bailey gathers the ball as Dino Sani closes in. Paolo Barison scored two and Dino Sani the other. Milan stars included Gianni Rivera and Cesare Maldini. Although Ipswich won the second leg 2-1 it was not enough.

Bill Baxter flies into a tackle on Dino Sani, but he was just too late. The Brazilian found the net with this shot. Ken Malcolm is the Ipswich defender on the right. The circles on the picture are raindrops that fell on the lens of the camera.

Paolo Barison (right) heads his second goal for Milan after getting the better of Larry Carberry (number two) in the air.

In all their years as a professional club Ipswich Town prided themselves on one of the best playing surfaces in the land. Much of the credit must go to head groundsman Freddie Blake (left) who put in so many hours in his efforts to attain perfection during a career with the club between 1927 and 1970. Blake had many tales to tell from his long association with the club. There was a time in January 1939 when Portman Road was flooded four feet deep. The match with Reading was postponed and even the reserve game at Torquay was called off because efforts to collect the kit from the dressing rooms failed. Trainer Bob Thomson and Blake attempted to row a coracle into the ground but found that the entrance was blocked by a sleeper, which had been washed off the terracing at the Churchmans end. The players' wages could not be made up, although they received a temporary loan, which was handed to them at the Police Station.

Wally Gray, an Ipswich Town goalkeeper in the club's amateur days, pictured with a youthful David Rose who succeeded him as club secretary at Portman Road. At first Wally's office used to be in a converted wooden hut, which was shared with the manager of the day.

Three
See-Saw Seasons

Jackie Milburn introduced a lot of new faces, many of them Scottish, in his attempt to save the club from the drop into the Second Division. Try as he might Jackie could not find a consistent winning formula and the 1963/64 season included some hammerings, such as the 10-1 Boxing Day defeat at Fulham and the 9-1 drubbing at Stoke. Milburn's effort to blend Ramsey's ageing players with his own newcomers led to a team like the one pictured above in front of old dressing rooms with the veranda. From left to right, back row: John Compton, Jim Thorburn, Bill Baxter, Joe Davin, Jack Bolton, George Dougan. Front row: Joe Broadfoot, Doug Moran, Roy Stephenson, Gerry Baker, Jimmy Leadbetter.

Joe Broadfoot, the fastest winger Ipswich have ever fielded, shakes hands with skipper Andy Nelson after his signing from Millwall in October 1963. A Londoner who held a taxi licence in the city, Joe moved to Northampton Town in November 1965 but was back at Portman Road, under Bill McGarry, in February 1967. A good club cricketer, Joe was one of the characters in football. Welcoming him are, from left to right: Jimmy Leadbetter, Roy Walsh, John Compton, Frank Treacy, Larry Carberry and Dennis Thrower. Treacy later joined St Mirren where Doug Millward, one of Ramsey's players, became the first Englishman to manage a Scottish club. Treacy was a Catholic and Millward tells the story that when he scored the winner against Celtic he had to go to confession. Walsh was a skilful winger from Dedham while Thrower was an Ipswich-born half-back who served the club well.

Broadfoot gets in a cross having beaten Portsmouth's skipper Jimmy Dickinson for pace in a match at Portman Road in a 7-0 home win in November 1964.

The great Stanley Matthews made his only appearance at Portman Road for Stoke City in an FA Cup fourth round tie in January 1964. It was one week before his forty-ninth birthday and John Compton had the thankless task of marking him – no-one wanted to be the player who ended Matthews' great career with a rugged tackle. Gerry Baker was injured after nine minutes of that match which was before the days of substitutes. The ten men of Ipswich battled to a 1-1 draw but lost the replay at the Victoria Ground when a scuffed shot from Jimmy McIlroy put Stoke through. In February 1964 Ipswich trainer Jimmy Forsyth turned out for his 600th consecutive League match, against Arsenal.

Jack Bolton, with his father, when arriving at Ipswich Railway station to sign from Raith Rovers. Bolton, a central defender, followed Raith Rovers' goalkeeper Jim Thorburn to Portman Road after the Scottish club had been relegated with a sorry defensive record.

The board of directors at Portman Road and senior players in the brief reign of Jackie Milburn. From left to right, back row: Jim Thorburn, John Colrain, Ted Phillips, Andy Nelson, Dennis Thrower, Roy Bailey, Jack Bolton, Trevor Smith, Jim Nelson and Dave Bevis. Third row: Stanley Prendergast (assistant groundsman), Roy Stephenson, Frank Treacy, Danny Hegan, John Smith, Noel Kearney, Doug Moran and Ken Thompson. Second row: Charlie Cowie (reserve team trainer), Jimmy Forsyth (first team trainer), Ray Crawford, George Dougan, Bill Baxter, John Compton, Roy Walsh, Joe Davin, Ian May, Bobby Blackwood, Eddie Spearritt, Jimmy Leadbetter and John Elsworthy. Front row: Willie Kerr, Alistair Cobbold, Major Alfred Terry, John Cobbold (chairman), Jackie Milburn, Cecil Robinson, Wally Gray (club secretary), Freddie Blake (head groundsman). The relegation season of 1963/64 was pretty depressing. No-one dreamed that the pre-season victories at Grenchen in Switzerland, for the Uhren Cup, were to be the last away win for months. The departure of Ray Crawford to Wolves, an appalling away record and three missed penalties all contributed to the failure. The arrival of Gerry Baker and Joe Broadfoot were encouraging but Ramsey's old stagers did not readily accept Milburn's new players. Furthermore, Milburn's discipline was lax and his tactical awareness questionable. The 10-1 trouncing at Fulham was an embarrassment although dense fog, which drifted in along the banks of the Thames only a few minutes after the final whistle, might have saved the day! Milburn planned for a quick return from the Second Division. He signed Mick McNeil, an England international defender, from Middlesbrough. He was only twenty-four years old and had 9 full England caps as well as being captain of the Under 23 national side. Frank Brogan, once a reserve for Scotland, joined from Celtic but Doug Moran refused terms and returned home to play for Dundee United. John Compton moved to Bournemouth. Northumberland Schoolboys' centre-half Derek Jefferson signed apprentice forms in May 1964. In his message to the fans Jackie Milburn wrote: 'Last season can only be termed as a most unfortunate one but, without dwelling on the facts too much, here's hoping that our education has been furthered and lessons have been learned'. Sadly for Milburn, the start of the following season was little better than what had gone before.

On 8 September 1964 Jackie Milburn resigned. Five matches had produced a single point, five goals had been leaked at home to Preston and away to Coventry. Then Norwich won 2-1 at Carrow Road. It was time to quit, although John Cobbold begged him to stay. The height of the Ipswich Town depression came in the autumn of 1964 when, having been relegated from the First Division, they sank to the very foot of the Second Division. Milburn's sorry record was: played 65, won 17, drawn 14, lost 34; goals for 99, goals against 149. On the day Milburn resigned Billy Baxter demanded a transfer. He delivered his letter to chairman John Cobbold saying: 'I don't see any future for me at Portman Road'. There was big trouble in the dressing room, so much so that John Cobbold broke one of his cardinal rules by addressing the players himself. Afterwards he said: 'I hope I have sorted out an undercurrent of feeling mainly with regard to the wage structure. The board have decided to revert to the old wages policy whereby all members of the first team are on the same money while they are in the side. This has worked very well in the past'. It was at this time that Cobbold, in rejecting Baxter's transfer request, said: 'We are manager-less, almost pointless and cannot afford to be Baxter-less'. *Pictured above:* Bill McGarry was appointed manager and took charge of a team in turmoil. He was just the disciplinarian needed to sort out the problems, although not everyone was happy with his abrupt manner. At a stormy shareholders' meeting Ken Brightwell, the supporters' choice, was invited onto the board.

Bill McGarry had been at Portman Road only a few weeks when his side responded with a 7-0 home victory over Portsmouth. *Above*: Gerry Baker testing Pompey goalkeeper John Milkins with Jimmy Dickinson and Alex Wilson in the background. *Below*: Danny Hegan scores one of his two goals. The other Town marksmen were hat-trick hero Frank Brogan, Baker and Joe Broadfoot.

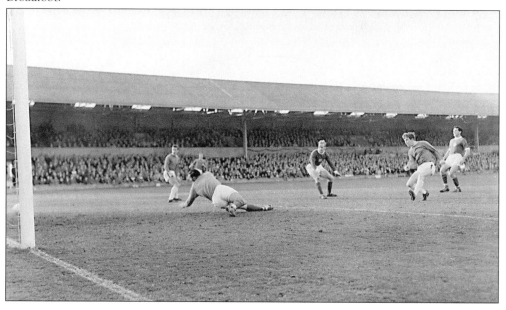

Bill McGarry was a manager who meant business. He shook the club from top to bottom. 'If they're not with me, then they are against me,' was his view on players and directors alike. He did not stand on ceremony. The language behind closed door was often blue. Although Bill Baxter (left) was the captain, players like Ken Hancock, Billy Houghton, John O'Rourke, Peter Morris, Tommy Carroll and Danny Hegan all played key roles in the Second Division Championship success.

Bill McGarry in jovial mood celebrating in style with his players. There were plenty of champagne corks popping after promotion was secured back into the First Division. The season also saw the emergence of youngsters like Derek Jefferson, who wore contact lenses on the field and spectacles off it, and Colin Viljoen, who scored a hat-trick in a 4-3 win at Norwich. Cyril Lea was now coaching the side.

There was the usual celebration as Ipswich Town returned to Division One. The open-topped bus shown here has Bill McGarry, his first team coach Sammy Chung and chairman John Cobbold in the back row. Then come Bobby Hunt, Colin Harper, Mick McNeil and Cyril Lea. Chief scout Reg Tyrrell is with the hat looking at the camera (Reg was always publicity conscious, especially with regard to the youngsters he brought in 'from down the line'). Prominent in the front are, from left to right: Bill Baxter, goalkeeper Ken Hancock (who was entrusted not to drop the cup), Ray Crawford, Danny Hegan, Tommy Carroll, Frank Brogan and John O'Rourke (who seems ready for rain). Partially obscured are Ron Wigg, Derek Jefferson (with glasses) and Billy Houghton (behind Crawford). The following November McGarry dropped a bombshell. He resigned to join Wolverhampton Wanderers where he declared there was 'more potential'.

Four
Robson's Glory Years

Bobby Robson was by no means Ipswich Town's first choice to succeed Bill McGarry. Once it was decided that caretaker Cyril Lea lacked the experience Ipswich went for Frank O'Farrell and then Billy Bingham. Both turned the job down. Robson, who had been recommended by Chelsea manager Dave Sexton, was something of a last resort and only clinched the job because he impressed the directors so much at his interview. How wonderfully well it all worked out! After an unsteady start, when the board stood by him, Robson moulded Ipswich Town into a power in European football. He is pictured here at the height of his triumphs holding the UEFA Cup in 1981.

Robson's Ipswich needed a few years to consolidate at the top level while the board resolutely backed their manager in times of stress. This photograph shows action from a 1-1 draw at Crystal Palace in November 1971. Derek Jefferson (nicknamed Chopper) is on the ball, Rod Belfitt is number nine and Johnny Miller number eleven. Selhurst Park has seen considerable development since those days.

One of the first players to leave after Robson's arrival was Ray Crawford, who signed for Charlton Athletic in March 1969. Eddie Firmani watches his new striker put pen to paper. Crawford had scored 16 goals in 30 First Division games. Later he was to star for Colchester United when they performed a giant-killing feat to knock Leeds United out of the FA Cup at Layer Road. Danny Hegan moved to West Bromwich with Ian Collard signed in part-exchange. Joe Broadfoot retired with a knee injury.

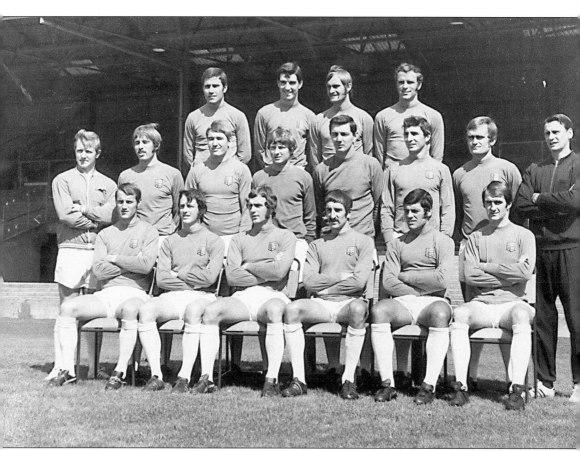

One of Robson's earlier squads featured the experienced duo, Jimmy Robertson and Frank Clarke, whose timely signings before the transfer deadline in 1970 staved off the threat of relegation. From left to right, back row: Colin Viljoen, Mick Lambert, Mick Mills, Tommy Carroll (who, with Baxter, became involved in a much-publicised scuffle with Robson that led to the departure of both players). Middle row: Cyril Lea (coach), Colin Harper, Derek Jefferson, Laurie Sivell, David Best, Mick McNeil, Bobby Hunt and Bobby Robson (manager). Front row: Bill Baxter, Jimmy Robertson (from Arsenal), Ian Collard (who had played for West Bromwich in the 1968 FA Cup final), Frank Brogan, Peter Morris, Frank Clarke (from QPR).

In September 1970 Ipswich made the trip to face Chelsea at Stamford Bridge. The 'goal that never was' incident was a talking point of the season. Alan Hudson's shot rebounded off the stanchion but referee Roy Capey awarded a goal. Normally ice-cool, goalkeeper David Best chased the referee to the half-way line, but all to no avail. Ipswich lost 2-1 and it's just as well that they managed to avoid relegation with seven points to spare. Clive Woods (white shirt, centre), a Norwich lad, was now well established in the side and should not be confused with Charlie Woods, also a winger, who later joined the coaching staff at Portman Road and held the post of assistant manager to Bobby Ferguson, John Duncan and John Lyall.

Another home produced player from the Norfolk-Suffolk border was Trevor Whymark (pictured left) from Burston. They were among those to show the value of a successful youth policy to a club like Ipswich Town. Whymark is pictured with the plaque awarded to him by Roma after he had scored four goals against their big rivals SS Lazio in the UEFA Cup. Geoff Hammond, father-in-law to England goalkeeper Richard Wright made his debut in that never-to-be-forgotten match at Chelsea. Hammond was born in Sudbury and was transferred to Manchester City in September 1974. Ipswich hung on in Division One in Robson's early years. They finished twelfth in 1968/69, eighteenth in 1969/70, nineteenth in 1971/71 and thirteenth in 1971/72. Then came lift-off time.

Allan Hunter was signed from Blackburn Rovers in September 1971 with Bobby Bell going the other way in part-exchange. The Northern Ireland international was a commanding presence in the centre of defence. At first he played alongside Derek Jefferson, before helping Kevin Beattie and John Wark develop their careers.

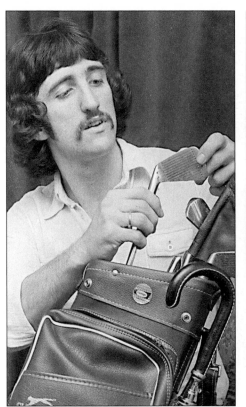

On 30 October 1972 Robson upset the fans with a deal that let Rod Belfitt (right) move to Everton in part-exchange for twenty-one year old David Johnson (left) who was little known away from Merseyside. Belfitt had scored five goals in the previous seven games. Johnson, though, combined brilliantly with Whymark and completed another piece of the Robson jigsaw.

David Johnson produces a spectacular scissors kick against Liverpool watched by Ian Collard and Kevin Beattie. It was the first season that the club adopted the Suffolk Punch as their badge instead of the town coat of arms. It was a great season for the club. They took fourth place in Division One behind Liverpool, Arsenal and Leeds United and won the Texaco Cup with two-leg victories over St Johnstone, Wolverhampton Wanderers, Newcastle United and, to cap it all, Norwich City – there were gates of 29,700 at Portman Road and 35,798 at Carrow Road for this epic East Anglia clash. Bryan Hamilton became well established on the right-wing after being signed from Linfield, where he had been a part-timer, the previous season. That meant that Jimmy Robertson could be transferred to Stoke City for £80,000. Ipswich also won the FA Youth Cup, beating Chelsea in the semi-final and Bristol City in a two-leg final. At the celebrations chairman John Cobbold told the parents of the team to retire to bed and produce another side for seventeen years time!

Ipswich were brimful of confidence at the start of 1973/74 season but being paired with the mighty Real Madrid in the first round of the UEFA Cup was daunting. Skipper Mick Mills (right) gives his colleagues, as well as manager Bobby Robson and coach Cyril Lea, a lesson in elementary Spanish for footballers. The first leg was at Portman Road and only the brilliance of Real goalkeeper Garcia Remon prevented Ipswich building up a convincing lead. By the end Ipswich had to settle for a single goal advantage when left-back Rubinan deflected a shot from Mills into his own net. There was controversy when referee Stanislav Eksztajn collapsed with a leg injury. He claimed to have been hit by a missile from the crowd although it seemed he had collided with a Real player. Nonetheless, Ipswich was fined £685 by a UEFA Commission. Colin Viljoen, the South African who secured an English passport and went on to win two caps under Don Revie in 1975, effectively shadowed West German international Gunter Netzer.

Perhaps there was a degree of psychological manipulation from Real Madrid when they invited the Ipswich Town players to look at their trophy room at the Bernabeu Stadium. Colin Viljoen, Bryan Hamilton and Mick Lambert look at more than 3,000 trophies. The Town players were unconcerned. They went on to dominate the second leg and quieten a crowd of 80,000. Ipswich went on the attack, which surprised the Spaniards who were used to opponents defending in depth. Real were without the injured Netzer and Amancio. Then midfield general Pirri was carried off with a broken knee cap. Viljoen was the star of a great Ipswich show and it was clear that Robson's players were making a big impact.

SS Lazio were the next opponents. They were famed for one of the most solid defences in Europe, but Mick Lambert made most of the openings and Trevor Whymark scored all four goals in the first leg at Portman Road, which led to Lazio's rivals, Roma, presenting him with an award. This inflamed feelings amongst Lazio fans and was partly to blame for the riot that followed Ipswich's 4-2 defeat, but aggregate win, in the Olympic Stadium. The Ipswich players stayed in the safety of the dressing room for two hours before going to a restaurant out of the city because hooligans were waiting outside their hotel. Colin Viljoen, Bryan Hamilton and David Johnson are pictured (above) at the restaurant well after midnight. Lazio were fined £1,500 and banned from European football for one year as a sequel to this night of disgrace.

George Knights was a key man in the Supporters Club for many years.

Ipswich went on to beat stylish Dutch club FC Twente Enschede in the third round. The team from Holland included Dutch international goalkeeper Piet Schrijvers and Under 23 midfield man Frans Thijssen, who was later to become a star at Portman Road. The picture shows Allan Hunter, Mick Mills and Kevin Beattie (kneeling) with pennants from the clubs Ipswich had so far overcome.

Ipswich Town used to have four ball boys on duty at every home match. It was a task many young followers hoped to perform. The picture shows the day a certain young Keith Deller (top left), later to become world darts champion, was given his opportunity. The other youngsters were Colin Kredewolf (standing), Terry Page and Michael Shorten.

Kevin Beattie, compared by many to the late Duncan Edwards of Manchester United, was PFA Young Footballer of the Year. Here he stands before the microphone to thank his fellow professionals after receiving the award from England boss Don Revie. By the spring of 1974 Ipswich had gone out of the UEFA Cup after a penalty shootout in Leipzig, but only after Mick Mills had been sent off in the 40th minute, experiencing what he described as 'the worst moment of his career'. At the end of the best of five penalties the sides were still level. Then it was sudden death. Leipzig's Moldt scored. All the pressure was on Allan Hunter whose shot was saved near the foot of the post. However, Ipswich finished fourth in Division One so they were back in the UEFA Cup again.

Laurie Sivell was the first choice goalkeeper in 1974/75 when Ipswich finished third behind Derby County and Liverpool, just a couple of points short of the title. He is pictured here looking at yachts at Oulton Broad, near his home. It was a season when interest in Europe ended on away goals against FC Twente but for once Ipswich had a spectacular run in the FA Cup. Wins over Wolves, Liverpool (the holders) and Aston Villa set up a battle royal with Leeds United in the sixth round. There were no goals at Portman Road, it was 1-1 at Elland Road after extra-time and another stalemate at Leicester set up a third replay at Filbert Street. It was sensational. Ipswich won 3-2 with the best memories being of a spectacular curling shot from Clive Woods and the debut of seventeen year old John Wark thrown in at the deep end in a crisis. Then came heartbreak. A semi-final replay against West Ham at Stamford Bridge will be remembered by disillusioned Town fans for the goal from Bryan Hamilton that was ruled out by referee Clive Thomas. It was also during this season that Allan Hunter rejected a £200,000 move to Leicester and goalkeeper Paul Cooper was signed from Birmingham City.

Trevor Kirton has spent much of his working life with the club. He became coach driver and kit manager after Ipswich were so impressed with Lazio's club coach that they decided to have one themselves. Now he is purchasing and stadium manager.

Brian Talbot, born and bred in Ipswich, was a late developer – so much so that he was almost allowed to move to Bournemouth before he had established a first team place. He scored 31 goals in 227 first team game before a move to Arsenal. He won 6 England caps (5 while at Ipswich), 2 England B caps and a single Under 21 cap. He is pictured here with some of his England gear.

Paul Cooper established himself as first choice goalkeeper after Ipswich went down 3-0 at home to Newcastle United on the opening day of the season. It was the first time they had lost an opening home match since 1959. Cooper and George Burley (below), who between them totalled 82 League appearances in the 1975/76 season are seen here in the thick of the action. Ipswich finished in sixth place in Division One and missed out on Europe for the following season because Southampton won the FA Cup (so Manchester United took the final UEFA place). During the campaign, Brian Talbot broke his leg for a third time and Bryan Hamilton, top marksman in November, was sold to Everton for £40,000. Laurie Sivell was recalled for the away fixture at Aston Villa, diving at Andy Gray's feet to save a certain goal in the match: he lost teeth and needed eleven stitches round his mouth. In the UEFA Cup Ipswich overcame Feyenoord but went out to Bruges despite taking a three-goal advantage to Belgium.

Paul Mariner (left) above joined Ipswich Town in October 1976 from Plymouth Argyle in a deal that sent striker Terry Austin and defender John Peddelty to Devon. Mariner was all set to sign for West Ham until Ipswich intervened at the last moment. There was also competition for the player from West Bromwich. Mariner, who started his career as a part-timer with Chorley, had attracted Bobby Robson's attention some time before. It was a season when Ipswich were not in Europe, had an early exit from cup competitions but ended in third place in Division One. Patrick Cobbold replaced his brother John as club chairman.

John Peddelty joined Plymouth but had suffered a depressed fracture in a reserve match the previous season. A similar injury put him out of the game so he joined the Police force and is pictured in blue, albeit not the blue of Ipswich Town.

Forget the League in 1977/78 season – it was the Year of the Horse when Ipswich Town won the FA Cup against Arsenal at Wembley. A poor final placing of eighteenth in the First Division was the outcome of a crop of injuries. The early part of the season had UEFA excitement at Landskrona Bois, Las Palmas and then Barcelona. Ipswich took a 3-0 lead to the Nou Camp Stadium against Johan Cruyff and company only to lose out on penalties for the second time in three years. The picture shows, from left to right: Paul Cooper, Mick Mills and Clive Woods taking a stroll in Las Palmas. All clearly found it warmer than they thought when they left their hotel.

Kevin Beattie was a key man for Ipswich and, but for injury, would have been an England regular for a great many years. In 1977/78 he underwent a cartilage operation – and was playing again in twenty-five days, which was an amazing recovery. His knee, though, continued to cause him problems. He did not play a League match between 8 October and 18 March, but he turned out in the home leg against Barcelona on 23 November. Another serious injury that season came at Norwich on Boxing Day when Trevor Whymark was stretchered off with damaged knee ligaments that cost him his place in the FA Cup final. Even so, Margaret Thatcher, one of the guests at Wembley, is said to have commented at the end 'The Ipswich number ten, Trevor Whymark, played well' – Whymark's name being in the official programme. Another Wembley story was that Lady Blanche Cobbold, president of Ipswich Town FC, was invited to meet Labour Prime Minister Jim Callaghan but replied: 'I'd rather have a gin and tonic'.

Ipswich Town's FA Cup run started with a 2-0 win at Cardiff and a 4-1 home victory over Hartlepool in the fourth round. Then came a tricky hurdle against Bristol Rovers at Eastville in the snow when Ipswich rode their luck and forced a replay with a couple of goals from Robin Turner. The replay was no problem with a 3-0 success, which led to a sixth round tie against Millwall at The Den. Bryan Hamilton was captain of the London side, whose fans went on the rampage. They invaded the pitch in the first half when play was suspended for eighteen minutes. There was trouble at the end as well, but Ipswich won 6-1 with a hat-trick from Paul Mariner. The picture shows Paul Cooper blocking a Millwall shot with his foot. George Burley, who opened the scoring, is the Ipswich player running back. In the semi-final Ipswich took on West Bromwich at Highbury. When Brian Talbot put Ipswich ahead after eight minutes he accidentally clashed heads with John Wile who carried on gallantly with blood seeping through a bandage round his forehead. Ipswich went on to win 3-1 and prepare themselves for their big day at Wembley Stadium.

Ipswich Town made Sopwell House Hotel at St Albans their Wembley headquarters. David Geddis and George Burley relax the day before the final.

The Ipswich fans, or at least those fortunate enough to secure tickets, were out in force with various banners. They were many magic moments for everyone connected with Portman Road.

Anxious moments as Bobby Robson leads out his Ipswich Town team, who started as underdogs.

Alan Sunderland (number 8), who was later to sign for Ipswich Town while Bobby Ferguson was manager, carries the ball towards the Ipswich goal, but Mick Mills has the move covered.

Clive Woods, considered by many to be the man of the match, puts in his cross despite the challenge of David O'Leary. Liam Brady, the Arsenal midfield general, is in the background.

A narrow shave for the Gunners' goal as Pat Jennings, in full flight, makes a marvellous save to prevent George Burley from opening the scoring with a header.

Roger Osborne (7) breaks the deadlock after 77 minutes. Willie Young blocked a cross from David Geddis and Osborne struck home a left-foot shot to become an Ipswich legend.

Mick Mills with the FA Cup, surrounded by players and coaches. Clive Woods holds the plinth. Facing the camera are, from left to right, standing: Roger Osborne, Mick Mills, Brian Talbot (who won an FA Cup winners' medal with Arsenal the following year), Clive Woods, substitute Mick Lambert, coach Bobby Ferguson and Russell Osman (who narrowly missed out on playing when Allan Hunter and Kevin Beattie passed late fitness tests). Seated: Paul Mariner, John Wark, George Burley, David Geddis.

Allan Hunter and Kevin Beattie, Ipswich Town's powerful central defenders, were not sure of playing until the morning of the match. Here, they are clasping their winners' medals with smiling coach Cyril Lea in between.

Roger Osborne and Paul Mariner parade the FA Cup round the Wembley touchline. These were euphoric moments for Ipswich supporters.

Home again, Mick Mills and Roger Osborne show the FA Cup to Ipswich fans outside the Town Hall after a tour of the town in an open-topped bus.

The players on the Town Hall steps with a placard saying 'Kevin Beattie walks on water' held by Kevin himself, complete with cigarette.

Ipswich director Murray Sangster and chairman John Cobbold are all smiles with manager Bobby Robson before the reception at the Town Hall given by the mayor, David Myer.

The tour of the town attracted an estimated 100,000 people to line the streets. There were even people watching from the rooftops.

Time moves on. Twenty years after the FA Cup final there was a players' reunion. Some of those present included, from left to right: Brian Talbot, George Burley, Roger Osborne, Laurie Sivell, Mick Lambert, Ron Gray (scout), John Wark, Mick Mills, Allan Hunter, Kevin Beattie.

David Johnson (in the background) returns to Portman Road in a Liverpool shirt. He is watching as his successor at Ipswich, Paul Mariner, wins a high ball.

Ipswich came back to earth with a bump at the start of 1978/79 with a 5-0 defeat against Nottingham Forest in the FA Charity Shield. There were big changes afoot. Brian Talbot moved to Arsenal for £450,000 and Trevor Whymark joined Vancouver Whitecaps. In came two talented Dutchmen, Arnold Muhren (on left of picture) and Frans Thijssen (right). The Ipswich style was changed to accommodate these skilful players with John Wark becoming a prolific goalscorer from midfield and also taking the penalties. It was a season when Robson was rebuilding. Ipswich finished sixth in the First Division, Eric Gates and Alan Brazil were breaking onto the scene, and Russell Osman became established. Ipswich went out in the sixth round of the FA Cup at home to Liverpool. In the European Cup Winners' Cup they disposed of AZ 67 Alkmaar and SW Innsbruck only to lose to Barcelona on away goals before a crowd of 100,000.

After the Wembley triumph, Bobby Robson strengthened his squad with new signings (Muhren, Thijssen and O'Callaghan) and promotion from the youth ranks (Brazil, Osman, Butcher, Gates and McCall). From left to right, back row: Alan Brazil, Paul Mariner, Russell Osman, Terry Butcher, Laurie Sivell, Paul Cooper, Frans Thijssen, Kevin Steggles, Allan Hunter, Arnold Muhren. Front row: Bobby Robson (manager), Eric Gates, John Wark, Mick Mills, Kevin Beattie, Kevin O'Callaghan, Steve McCall, Bobby Ferguson (coach).

Russell Osman, who played schoolboy rugby for England, emerged as a classy defender. He is seen in action against Bristol City with Tom Ritchie in the background.

Bobby Robson has words with Eric Gates, whose skill playing just behind the strikers and ability to dribble the ball into the penalty area caused massive problems for First Division defences. In 1979/80 Ipswich finished in third place in the League behind Liverpool and Manchester United. They went out of the FA Cup in the sixth round at Everton and lost to Grasshoppers on the away goal rule once again in the second round of the UEFA Cup, having overcome Skeid Oslo.

Paul Mariner dives in against Stoke City goalkeeper Peter Fox at the Victoria Ground, which has now been replaced by the Britannia Stadium. Arnold Muhren and Mick Mills are in the background.

What a season it was for Ipswich in 1980/81. Runners-up to Aston Villa in Division One and in the semi-final of the FA Cup, they went on to win the UEFA Cup and bring more joy to Ipswich fans. The triumph in Europe takes pride of place – what a performance it turned out to be. The UEFA Cup seldom throws up an easy tie. The visit of Aris Salonika, to whom cynical defence seemed to come naturally, saw John Wark start to make an impact as a scorer from midfield. He scored four against the Greeks, who had sweeper Firos sent off, but three came from the penalty spot. It was tense out in Greece, with Town trailing 3-0 on the night and a 40,000 crowd both noisy and hostile. However, an Eric Gates strike took the sting out of the tie in the 75th minute with a goal, which allowed Town fans to breathe more easily. This picture shows a scene familiar to Aris – a booking for their centre-half who is pleading innocence. Kevin Beattie, a colossus, was the man who put fear into the Bohemians of Prague. He appeared as substitute to score Town's third goal from 25 yards to make the tally 3-0 in the home leg. It was just as well that he did. The Bohemians fought back to win the second leg 2-0 so it was touch and go.

Paul Mariner took over as captain from the injured Mick Mills. Here, he exchanges pennants with the St Etienne skipper at Portman Road. The pairing with the Poles of Widzew Lodz had looked daunting on paper. They were unbeaten in their league that season and had already disposed of Manchester United and Juventus in the UEFA Cup. Three more goals from the amazing Wark helped Ipswich to a 5-0 win in the home leg so the visit to Poland, where there was ice and snow, was less of an ordeal than it would normally have been. The Poles were probably more concerned at the time about a possible invasion from Russia than a mere football match. It was not until the following March that Ipswich took on St Etienne, who had crushed Hamburg 6-0 on aggregate in the previous round. St Etienne, known as *Les Verts*, had lost only one European tie in 30 at home but were shaken rigid by Ipswich, who were in no way prepared to buckle under against the likes of Michel Platini and Dutchman Johnny Repp. The 4-1 away win was a classic performance and the tie was as good as over.

Mick Mills leads his players out for their semi-final second leg tie in Cologne. Goalkeeper Paul Cooper looks pensive as he takes to the field. FC Cologne had stars aplenty. Goalkeeper Harald Schumacher, Rainer Bonhof, Dieter Muller and Pierre Littbarski were household names in West Germany. They also fielded Swiss international Rene Botheron and England's Tony Woodcock. Ipswich took a 1-0 lead to Germany thanks to another goal from Wark, but would it be enough for a Town side now feeling the effects of a hectic programme and whose League challenge was falling apart at the seams? Ipswich were leg weary and spirits were low when they left for Germany. On the previous Saturday they had lost 2-0 against Arsenal at Highbury and on the Monday they had gone down 1-0 in an East Anglian derby match at Norwich. The Cologne game was on the Wednesday, so how could the Ipswich coaching staff bring fresh life into tired limbs? Training was unnecessary at that stage of the season. It was a case of resting the muscles and freshening the mind. The German Press helped by quoting bragging Cologne players as being super confident, but they were amazed to find the Ipswich squad enjoying themselves at a theme park the day before the match. History records that Terry Butcher scored the only goal of the night in Cologne. The Germans were stunned and Ipswich had reached a two-leg final against AZ 67 Alkmaar.

A moment for England and Ipswich Town captain Mick Mills to savour as he exchanges pennants with West German international goalkeeper Harald Schumacher at Portman Road. Schumacher will be forever infamous for his foul on French player Battiston in the semi-final of the 1982 World Cup. Dutch team AZ 67 Alkmaar chose the Olympic Stadium in Amsterdam for the second match, Ipswich winning the tie 5-4 on aggregate. It seemed fitting that a Dutchman, Frans Thijssen, should score a goal in each leg. In that UEFA Cup run John Wark's 14 goals equalled the record for European competition set by Jose Altafini of AC Milan in 1962/63 (when, ironically, they knocked out Ipswich Town in the second round).

Ipswich conceded four goals in the second leg in Holland and on this occasion Paul Cooper is well beaten. Later Mick Mills revealed that Bobby Robson had put extra pressure on the players by suggesting that, if Ipswich did not win, he might quit the club.

All is well in the dressing room at the end with, from left to right: Kevin Beattie, Paul Cooper, Terry Butcher and Frans Thijssen weary but overjoyed.

John Wark and Paul Mariner kiss the UEFA Cup, the first important European trophy to be won by Ipswich Town.

It's a rainy evening judging by Alan Brazil's umbrella and the hood being worn by Eric Gates. It did not dampen the enthusiasm of the crowds, however, who turned out in force to welcome Ipswich Town's warriors back home from their European conquest.

Never before had one club scooped the pool of individual awards. The Football Writers' Association chose Frans Thijssen (left of picture) as their footballer of the year, the first foreigner to win since Bert Trautmann. Furthermore, Mick Mills was runner-up with John Wark in third place.

The Professional Footballers' Association award went to John Wark. He is pictured below sending the Stoke City goalkeeper the wrong way from the penalty spot. Thijssen and Paul Mariner followed Wark in the voting. It was the first time that players of the same club have come in the top three. Wark was nominated as the European Young Player of the Year. It was heady stuff. Any bitterness over missing out on both top domestic prizes was soothed by the memorable triumph in the UEFA Cup.

Bobby Robson's final full season at Portman Road was 1981/82 when, once again, his formidable team were runners-up to Liverpool in the First Division and reached the semi-finals of the Football League Cup, going out over two legs to Liverpool. Robson moved to Lancaster Gate following in the footsteps once trodden by Alf Ramsey. He looks happy as he holds England shirts, but little did he bargain for vitriolic personal attacks from sections of the national press.

Five
Seasons of Struggle

On 1 September 1982 Bobby Robson officially started his duties with the Football Association as England manager. He recommended that his first team coach, Bobby Ferguson (pictured conducting an interview), should be his successor. Ferguson, aged forty-four, had been with the club for eleven years. The team was beginning to break up and, in addition, the board had decided to increase the capacity of the Pioneer Stand without a viable funding plan. Arnold Muhren had reached the end of his contract and had negotiated a move to Manchester United on a free transfer. At the end of that season Frans Thijssen, whose form had been disappointing, left to join Vancouver Whitecaps. In November 1982 Mick Mills became a Southampton player at the age of thirty-three.

In 1983/84 Ipswich were twelfth in Division One with many of the old guard still going strong. Ferguson promoted youngsters like Mark Brennan, Jason Dozzell, Mich D'Avray and Ian Cranson at the same time as signing the experienced Dutchman Romeo Zondervan (pictured left) from West Bromwich. This led to an incident at Old Trafford on 7 May 1984. Ferguson collected the Manchester United team sheet from the referee's room. He had his head down studying it as he walked into the dressing room. He started to talk tactics without looking up when he discovered he was in the wrong dressing room – he had seen Reme Moses and confused him with Romeo Zondervan! No wonder United boss Ron Atkinson was somewhat taken aback. Ferguson told his own players what had happened, which had the effect of easing their tension.

Ipswich went out to win with goals from Mich D'Avray and loan player Alan Sunderland (pictured centre). On loan from Arsenal, Sunderland did well enough to be given a contract for the following season. It was a sad season with the death of John Cobbold at the age of fifty-six. At one time Ipswich were in the bottom three in the table and the position was beginning to look hopeless until five wins and a draw in the last six games changed everything. Earlier in the season Paul Mariner (to Arsenal for £150,000) and John Wark (to Liverpool for £450,000) had moved on. Both had demanded wage increases at a time when gates were falling.

A meeting of two South Africans. Mich D'Avray (left), the Ipswich striker, secured a British passport and played for England's Under 21 side. He is faced by Manchester United goalkeeper, Gary Bailey, the son of Roy Bailey who kept goal for Ipswich in the glory days under Alf Ramsey.

Trevor Putney, a chirpy Londoner who upset manager Bobby Ferguson when he got on the club tannoy while a reserve match was in progress and sent a message to goalkeeper Mark Grew with whom he was in business with a second-hand shop in the town. Putney was transferred to Norwich in a deal that brought experienced John Deehan to Portman Road.

Bobby Ferguson's young guns, from left to right: Trevor Putney, Mark Brennan, Steve McCall and Frank Yallop (who went on to win many international caps for Canada).

Ian Cranson, one of the hardest tacklers ever to put on an Ipswich shirt, played alongside the dependable Terry Butcher who was the cornerstone of the Ipswich defence. In 1984/85 Ipswich stayed up once again. They had a bit of excitement in the Milk Cup when they reached the semi-final, which they lost over two legs to Norwich City.

Jason Dozzell became the youngest ever Ipswich Town player and the youngest to score in the First Division at the age of 16 years and 57 days. Still a pupil at Chantry High School in Ipswich, he scored against Coventry City after being introduced as substitute. Manager Bobby Ferguson is shown here setting him off on his first team career. In 1985/86 Ipswich dropped out of the First Division but only after a great fight. They lost Russell Osman to Leicester for £200,000 and Eric Gates, and then George Burley, to Sunderland for £150,000 and £50,000 respectively. Terry Butcher suffered a series of injuries while Steve McCall broke his toe against Manchester United and missed ten games. At the turn of the year Alan Sunderland hurt his back in a road accident. Into the club came Ian Atkins and Nigel Gleghorn, while Mick Stockwell made his debut.

The urgent need for funds for the Pioneer Stand development meant that star defender Terry Butcher had to be sold. He started as a sixteen year old raw recruit but left as an established England international. The fee of £725,000 from Glasgow Rangers seemed a give-away even though it was a record paid by a Scottish club to an English one. However, Ferguson had no money to spend and, despite the goalscoring of Kevin Wilson from Derby County (pictured left), Ipswich could not bounce back straight away, although they made the play-offs.

John Deehan, signed from Norwich City in a deal that took Trevor Putney to Carrow Road, was nearing the end of his career after spells in the Midlands, notably with Aston Villa. Later he went into management and coaching.

Failure to beat Charlton Athletic in the play-offs meant that Bobby Ferguson's contract was not renewed. The club lost a top-class coach and paid for dearly for a decision that was brought about by pressure from supporters. A shortlist of four was drawn up to take over. They were Keith Peacock of Gillingham, Ian Bowyer (who had just finished a distinguished playing career), coach Charlie Woods and John Duncan from Chesterfield. Duncan, a former Tottenham and Derby County striker, was appointed. He is pictured here with his best-known signing, Sergei Baltacha from Dynamo Kiev. Baltacha was a Soviet international sweeper – but never played in that position for Ipswich, which was almost beyond belief.

David Linighan was one of John Duncan's best signings. A member of a footballing family from Hartlepool, his elder brother Andy played for Norwich City, Arsenal and Crystal Palace. Linighan was strong in the air. He also owned a Staffordshire bull terrier, that on one occasion travelled to an away match leading to an amusing incident. Linighan shared a hotel room with John Wark and the dog was asleep at the end of Linighan's bed, but when Wark was taken short in the night every time he made as if to move to the bathroom the dog growled. Eventually Linighan woke up, quietened the animal, and all was well.

Mark Brennan, a talented left-footed player, was able to play at the highest level. He and Dozzell won England Under 21 caps but landed themselves in trouble with coach Dave Sexton when breaking a curfew in Toulon in 1987. Norwich City players Robert Rosario and Dale Gordon were in the same boat.

The Manor Ground at Oxford is the setting for this midfield tussle between Romeo Zondervan (left), now Ipswich Town's European scout, and Northern Ireland international Jim Magilton (on the ball) who joined Ipswich Town from Sheffield Wednesday in 1999.

David Lowe (left), who was signed from Wigan Athletic, gets in a shot against Wolves. Mark Venus (third player from the left) is playing for the Midland club. John Wark and Tony Humes are the other Ipswich players involved in the action.

Swimming is sometimes part of training, particularly for players trying to overcome injury. Chris Kiwomya, Jason Dozzell and Simon Milton are in the pool. Milton's signing from Bury Town was set up by Bobby Ferguson but completed by John Duncan.

John Duncan's long ball game led to a drop in gates at Portman Road when Ipswich were not prominent in the promotion battle. He was, however, keen to promote the club in the community and sent his players to train at a different school once a week. Here, the players are pictured with the youngsters.

Six
Lyall and McGiven

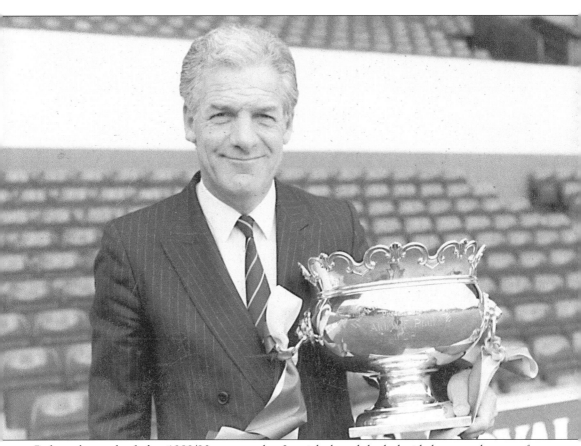

Before the end of the 1989/90 season the Ipswich board had decided on a change of management. Charlie Woods, whose title under John Duncan had changed from assistant manager to 'assistant to the manager' was designated to sound out John Lyall with whom he had worked as a scout for Bobby Robson in the World Cup in Italy in 1990. Lyall, pictured above, was working for Terry Venables at Tottenham at the time, following his departure from West Ham where he had been manager from 1974 to 1989. Lyall saw the Ipswich directors at Glemham Hall and accepted the job.

Lyall was a well-respected coach who revitalised the career of David Linighan by appointing him as captain. He worked well with Chris Kiwomya – whom he nicknamed 'Lino' because he was always on the floor. Kiwomya is shown here challenging the Oxford United goalkeeper at the Manor Ground.

A pensive John Lyall in the dugout has just said something to amuse physiotherapist David Bingham, who was brought to Portman Road by former boss John Duncan. Bingham had been at Wigan Athletic but was known to Duncan because his father, Revd John Bingham, was chaplain to Chesterfield Football Club, where Duncan had been in charge.

Mick McGiven was the man John Lyall seemed to be grooming as his successor at Portman Road. A good coach, McGiven did not enjoy his dealings with the media.

Steve Whitton was a shrewd signing by John Lyall from Sheffield Wednesday, but he had already impressed the Town boss when they were together at West Ham. Whitton often played as a wide target man and went on to play for and then manage Colchester United.

Ipswich won promotion to the Premiership under John Lyall at the end of 1991/92 season. The players are shown celebrating in the dressing room. In the foreground are: John Wark, Paul Goddard, Phil Whelan (with bottle), Steve Whitton, Jason Dozzell and Mick Stockwell.

There is sheer joy in the faces of Canadian goalkeeper Craig Forrest, marksman Chris Kiwomya and Jason Dozzell.

Mick Stockwell was voted player of the year by supporters in the 1992/93 season. He is holding the Harwich Rose Bowl proudly above his head. The versatile Stockwell gave Ipswich tremendous service before his move to Colchester United.

A happy Ipswich Town squad in the John Lyall era before they found themselves rather out of their depth in the Premiership, where they had to graft for every point. From left to right, back row: Craig Forrest, Gavin Johnson, Steve Whitton, Eddie Youds, Neil Thompson, Phil Whelan, Romeo Zondervan, Steve Palmer, Frank Yallop, Glen Pennyfather, John Wark, Neil Gregory. Front row: Mick Stockwell, Paul Goddard, Chris Kiwomya, David Linighan (captain), Jason Dozzell, Simon Milton, the mascot. Once promotion was achieved, with Lyall very much a tracksuit manager, he handed over much of the day-to-day training responsibility to coach Mick McGiven, who had been with him at West Ham.

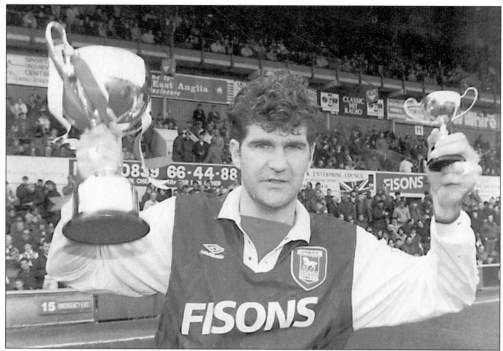

New players were signed for the effort to stay in the Premiership. One of these was Ian Marshall from Oldham Athletic who was keen for the opportunity to prove himself as a striker when Oldham boss Joe Royle wanted to play him as a central defender. Marshall became a popular figure at Portman Road.

Steve Sedgley was recruited from Tottenham Hotspur for £1 million. A skilful footballer, equally comfortable in defence as in midfield, Sedgley had excellent credentials, having won 11 England Under 21 caps while with Coventry City and then Spurs.

Bulgarian international Bontcho Guentchev (left) and Vlado Bozinoski (right) were signed from Bobby Robson's Sporting Lisbon. They are shown here being welcomed to Portman Road by coach Mick McGiven. Guentchev soon found himself in a storm over whether his past qualifications genuinely entitled him to a work permit. However, a letter signed by the president of the Bulgarian FA, stating that he had 16 A caps and had scored 6 goals was good enough for the authorities. There was bad feeling between the club and the local press when records suggested that he had just one cap at that stage against Sweden in a friendly match. Guentchev went on to play for Bulgaria in the World Cup in the United States. He was popular with the Ipswich fans and scored a hat-trick in an FA Cup tie against Grimsby Town. Little was seen of Bozinoski, an Australian with a European passport, at first team level.

Stuart Slater, a Suffolk lad, was a skilful on the ball but went to West Ham as a youngster, where he cut in to score a marvellous goal against Everton. He won 3 England Under 21 caps then moved to Celtic but became available. Lyall had worked with him before so plunged in, but it was a deal that never really worked out well for player or club.

Senior Ipswich Town players, from left to right: Paul Goddard, Steve Whitton, Mick Stockwell and David Linighan welcome Paul Mason into the fold from Aberdeen. Mason had the knack of scoring goals at the top level.

Ipswich Town needed to sell top players to generate funds. In August 1993 Jason Dozzell, a local Ipswich boy, joined Tottenham Hotspur for £1.9 million which kept the bank manager happy. Dozzell never really did himself justice with the London giants.

John Lyall and his assistant Charlie Woods ventured off to South America to recruit new talent. They returned with Uruguayan striker Adrian Paz, who was given a mountain to climb after being heralded as 'an old fashioned English centre forward'. In fact he turned out to be a skilful but lightweight player ideally suited to the wing.

Lyall also returned with Mauricio Taricco, a young Argentinian from Argentinos Juniors, who struggled on his debut in a League Cup tie at home to Bolton. Taricco needed time to settle down in England and soon became a popular defender who was sold to Tottenham Hotspur to help balance Ipswich Town's books.

Paul Goddard was a popular centre forward at QPR, West Ham, Newcastle United (where he received a tremendous reception when he returned in Ipswich colours) and Derby County. He was not so popular at Millwall, but that was because of his past Hammers' connection. After John Lyall resigned, Goddard, together with John Wark, had a spell as caretakers at Portman Road during a difficult time in the club's history.

Seven

George Burley Returns

John Lyall resigned and Mick McGiven went as well. Over Christmas 1994 came the news that George Burley, who had been at Colchester United only a few months, was to take over at Portman Road. Ipswich Town were already as good as doomed although there was talk of a fight back, especially after the club's first ever win at Liverpool. Burley's appointment led to a rift between Ipswich Town and Colchester United that had to be settled by the lawyers.

George Burley made a speedy impression when he first came to Portman Road after attending trials in Easter 1971. He had approached the club with some trepidation after being rejected by Leeds United. He was soon in the team that won the FA Youth Cup and was only seventeen years old when he made his debut against Manchester United at Old Trafford. It was Burley's first game and a farewell appearance for George Best. Note the difference between the leather balls of that decade and the lighter ones of today. *Above*: A young Burley together with Glenn Keeley, a central defender who later played for Newcastle United and Blackburn Rovers. *Left*: Burley arrives at Ipswich with fellow young Scot Kenny Taylor, who did not make the grade as a top professional footballer.

George Burley, having won an FA Cup winners' medal in 1978, is pictured with his proud parents Bill and Sadie. The following year Burley started his international career with Scotland. In all he won 11 full caps in 1979, 1980 and 1982. His playing career took him to Sunderland and Gillingham before a return to Scotland where he had a spell as player-manager at Ayr United.

Dale Roberts, a contemporary of George Burley's as a player, was his assistant manager at Ayr and the partnership has been cemented at Portman Road.

As Ipswich struggled in the Premiership during the second part of 1994/95 season, they set a record they could have done without. On 5 March 1995 the scoreline at Old Trafford read Manchester United 9 Ipswich Town 0. Ipswich suffered 29 defeats in 42 League games. They came up against all the top names in the land. The picture shows Dwight Yorke (no 18), then of Aston Villa, bearing down on Craig Forrest in the Ipswich goal. The Town defender was Chris Swailes who had started his career at Portman Road, moved into non-League but was recruited from Doncaster Rovers.

Charlie Woods became chief scout under George Burley. His many contacts in the game were invaluable.

Adam Tanner, an Essex lad who developed through the youth scheme, looked to have a great future when scoring the winner against Liverpool at Anfield. However, Adam's career ran into trouble with problems off the field. Here, he leaps higher than the others with Lee Chapman also in the thick of the action.

It is rare for a Cambridge University graduate to make the grade in professional football, but Steve Palmer was the exception. Ipswich spotted his potential when playing their annual match against the Light Blues at Fenners. Palmer had been with Brighton who let him go. A wholehearted defender, he moved to Watford for whom he played in the Premiership in the 1999/2000 season.

Simon Milton, whose transfer from Bury Town was set up by Bobby Ferguson then finalised by John Duncan, remained a loyal Ipswich Town player under Lyall and Burley. Here he challenges David Lowe of Leicester City (a former Ipswich star) with Danish international Claus Thomsen looking on.

Under George Burley's regime Ipswich Town had first to put their finances back on an even keel and continue to develop players through the youth policy. Players were sold and the production line was maintained. James Scowcroft from Stanton, now a former England Under 21 international and established target man, is shown here when on the bottom rung of the ladder playing a youth match against Fulham in 1993. Richard Wright and Kieron Dyer have been other notable successes. Wright and Dyer have both become full England internationals, the latter having moved to Newcastle United for a fee of £6 million that enabled the club to make a successful promotion challenge in the 1999/2000 season.

Signings also had to be made and Alex Mathie turned out to be a shrewd signing who possessed an eye for goal.

Ipswich Town fans seem to delight in any embarrassment that might befall their rivals from Norwich City. An afternoon they will never forget was in April 1996 when Bryan Gunn, the Canaries' goalkeeper, tried a hurried first time boot upfield from a back pass from Robert Ullathorne. The ball took a wicked bounce, Gunn missed it completely, and it rolled behind him into the goal. Gunn's expression tells the whole story while Canaries' number 11, Darren Eadie, can only hold his hands to his head in bewilderment and despair. Gus Uhlenbeek, though, is elated.

Ipswich Town have often looked to Holland for their players after the happy experiences with Arnold Muhren, Frans Thijssen and Romeo Zondervan. Then came the speedy Gus Uhlenbeek and the tricky Bobby Petta (above). Petta cost nothing from Feyenoord but Ipswich were anxious to secure a transfer fee if possible rather than let him go for nothing at the end of his contract under the Bosman ruling. Ipswich agreed a £500,000 fee with Barnsley but Petta, on the advice of his agent, was not interested. In the summer of 1999 he moved to Celtic on a good contract and also on a free transfer. This is sure to happen more and more in professional football where agents do almost all the negotiations. One can only wonder how the old-time managers like Bill Shankly and Brian Clough would have coped with the present day agents.

Shrewd signings at bargain prices have been one of the foundations of Ipswich Town's success in the second part of the nineties. Jamie Clapham (right), a Lincolnshire lad, was going nowhere in Tottenham's reserve team. He came on loan to Ipswich, impressed everyone, and was offered a contract. A left wing-back who is particularly strong going forward, Clapham was the supporters' player of the year in the spring of 1999.

David Johnson, the second striker of that name to become a Portman Road legend, looks bemused with his hands to his head. Johnson's electric pace has been a scourge to Division One defences since being signed from Bury in a deal that took defender Chris Swailes the other way. Johnson started with Manchester United and played in the same youth team as David Beckham.

Ipswich have had some cruel luck in Division One play-off semi-finals. *Above*: Sasa Ilic punches clear in the first leg against Charlton Athletic at Portman Road in May 1998. Charlton won the midfield battle and the tie overall. They overcame Sunderland in a thrilling final at Wembley. *Below*: The second leg against Bolton Wanderers at Portman Road in May 1999 reaches extra-time. Jim Magilton is having his thigh massaged, Matt Holland has a drink of water while Kieron Dyer (7) was making his farewell appearance at Portman Road before his £6 million move to Newcastle United. Ruud Gullit agreed the fee but Kieron was soon to be playing under the command of Bobby Robson.

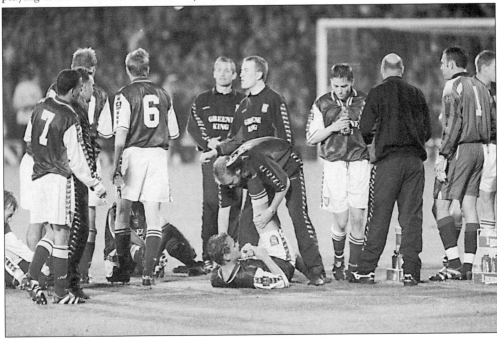

A good scouting network has been all-important to Ipswich Town over the years. The chief scout at the start of the new Millennium is Colin Suggett (above), who works with Romeo Zondervan on the Continent as well as with a network in Britain. Reg Tyrrell was the first effective Ipswich Town scout in the time of Bill McGarry, Ron Gray always had an eye for a top player while John Carruthers (right) was the club's Northern scout who was responsible for bringing Kevin Beattie to Portman Road. Kevin, of course, might have been a Liverpool player had someone from Anfield met him at Lime Street Stadium those many years ago.

Matt Holland, Ipswich Town's captain in succession to Tony Mowbray who handed over the armband when he became player-coach at the start of 1999/2000 season. Mowbray was only planning to play in an emergency. By October he was needed to hold together a defence that had started to leak goals. Holland, though, was an enthusiastic skipper who was rewarded for his excellent work by an international call-up by the Republic of Ireland. Holland hates to miss a game and his run of successive appearances, making light of injury worries, since he signed from Bournemouth for £700,000 was phenomenal. Mowbray became first team coach after Ipswich had used the experience of Bryan Hamilton, Stewart Houston and John Gorman before him. Holland leads by example and has developed a splendid rapport with the Ipswich supporters.

Ipswich faced Bolton in the Division One play-off semi-finals for the second time in as many years in May 2000. Ipswich fought back from a two-goal deficit at the Reebok Stadium and then won the day at Portman Road in a tussle that turned ugly. This photograph shows Jim Magilton being tripped by Robbie Elliott with Marcus Stewart, the club's £2.75 million record signing from Huddersfield Town, in close attendance. Stewart's signing, after protracted negotiations, was for £2.5 million with a further £250,000 to pay if Ipswich won promotion. He was hard hit by injury in his early weeks at Portman Road, but scored a wonderful goal at the Reebok Stadium to prove his value after David Johnson had gone off injured.

The award of a penalty to Ipswich Town just before the interval in the second leg of the Division One play-off semi-final against Bolton Wanderers caused a fracas that led to trouble for some of the Bolton players. Claus Jensen, who chose to sign for Charlton rather than Ipswich in the summer of 2000, is between Robbie Elliott and Jamie Clapham. Bolton lost much of their composure after this incident and were reduced to nine men when Mike Whitlow and, later, Elliott were sent off. Ipswich went on to win 5-3 after extra-time with a hat-trick from Jim Magilton (despite missing the spot kick that led to the trouble). Ipswich beat Barnsley 4-2 in the final at Wembley Stadium, which was one of the most exhilarating days in the club's history with around 37,000 Ipswich fans watching the action under the Twin Towers.

More joy on the Town Hall steps in Ipswich as the promoted players celebrate in front of massed fans. *Above*: Richard Naylor, who gave a gallant performance at Wembley Stadium despite the need for surgery on his knees, receives acclaim. *Below*: Marcus Stewart takes video footage of the big occasion from his vantage point on the rooftop of the coach. Stewart's arrival at Ipswich from Huddersfield proved vital to the promotion bid.

David Sheepshanks, the Ipswich Town chairman, and his manager George Burley achieved their goal of Premiership football in the spring of the year 2000. It was brought about by teamwork. Both are clearly delighted.